ISBN-10: 0-692-54229-9
ISBN-13: 978-0-692-54229-3

The WilderWay LLC
www.TheWilderWay.com

Printed in China

Our wild world awaits!
But first...

What is "Evolution"?

While evolution is a very complicated scientific topic, it can be thought of simply as:

"The changes within a species (a group of similar living things) over great amounts of time caused by passing traits from one generation to the next (parents to offspring)."

But this is still a bit complicated! So *Evolutionary Tales* aims to simplify things a little further and act as an introduction to the diverse world of evolution by showcasing what exactly this process can lead to: Wild and highly-adapted creatures of all shapes, sizes, and talents!

Now prepare to embark on a fantastic, but entirely-true journey, coming face to face with some of evolution's wildest products!

The Sword-billed Hummingbird

Deep in the forest,
Quite calm and quite dim,
There's a long, thin flower,
Hanging far out on a limb.

While it may seem strange,
So gangly and odd,
Its shape has purpose,
And it's quite good at its job!

For it has quite an interest,
In its tiny, winged friend.
And to lure him over,
A bright signal it sends.

With lightning-fast wing beats,
He flies like a dart!
Heading straight for the flower,
And the meal he will start.

It's a bird very different,
From most others around.
His body's quite small,
But his beak will astound!

Through the history of both,
They've evolved hand in hand.
A coevolution,
Where both benefit grand!

You see, the bird with its beak,
Can reach nectar to be found,
And the flower - on the bird,
Can deposit pollen all around.

One of the most wonderful friendships,
This world's ever heard.
The Passiflora mixta flower,
And the Sword-billed Hummingbird!

The Anglerfish

Dip below the ocean surface.
Sink down through its darkened depths.
Leave the light behind and witness,
The creatures that may scare to death!

But it's so hard to see down here,
In this lightless deep.
We're blind as a bat, and oblivious to,
All these waters keep.

But wait! What's that?
It's just the faintest of glow.
You see? Right there!
Watch it bob and flow.

Oh look, it's attached,
Like a small chandelier.
And there's something behind it,
Now the light makes it clear.

There are two eyes and some fins,
And the light hangs from its face.
It reflects off its teeth,
And we're frozen in place.

It's an Anglerfish,
And her name suits her well.
For she's the greatest of fishermen,
In the dark where she dwells.

But she owes her bright lure,
To a sort so evolved.
A colony of bacteria,
Reside in her bulb.

They're fed by the fish,
And in return, produce light.
So this fierce, toothy angler,
Can hunt out of sight!

The Birds of Paradise

When a habitat's full,
Of such a number of creatures,
How's one to stand out?
And display all their features?

For seeking a mate's,
An already difficult thing,
Vying with others,
And all competition they bring.

So how do you prove,
You're the best of the lot?
How do you strut,
And flaunt all you've got?

The Birds of Paradise certainly,
Seem to be in the know.
For when a female flies by,
The male's colors will show!

And what colors they are,
A true rainbow of flair!
Only the brightest will triumph,
And catch the fair female's stare!

While she may be quite drab,
Far from the male's sense of style,
She's the bird who decides,
So she'll take quite a while.

She'll let them dance, showing off.
She'll watch their intricate show.
But if their colors aren't perfect,
Off to the next bird she'll go.

For she seeks a mate who is fit,
Who can pass great genes to their young.
And from a clean bill of health,
Is where the bright colors have sprung!

The Sugar Glider

To climb up a gum tree,
Requires a daredevil-ish mind.
But to leap from its branches,
Takes a whole other kind!

But while most would plummet,
Straight below to the ground,
Our climber is skilled!
He's developed a softer way down.

As he leaps from his perch,
And as he falls ever faster,
His legs spread - extended,
As he dodges disaster!

Webbing appears,
Between each pair of paws.
Once climber, now flier,
As he pitches and yaws!

He descends with a glide,
Extra skin catching air.
Odd ones, Sugar Gliders,
With their flourish and flair.

They're Australian possums,
With "patagium" - the skin,
That extends between legs,
When gliding begins.

They can fall in this style,
For quite a long way,
To escape predators,
Or to catch their own prey!

Our glider readies to land.
He pulls his legs in tight.
The patagium folds up,
Until his next fearless flight!

The Archerfish

A bug on a branch,
Over water so still.
Sitting there, so relaxed,
As any bug will.

There's not a frog in the grass,
Nor birds in the trees.
No danger at all,
Or so it believes.

But below in the water,
Hides a hunter so fierce.
He readies to shoot,
And the surface to pierce.

His liquidy shot,
Rings out through the air.
Connects hard with the bug,
And leaves the branch bare.

In the water, now trapped,
The bug's hopelessly doomed.
All due to the fact,
Of the safety assumed.

But no tiny creature,
Is safe where he swims.
Archerfish have evolved,
To shooting branches and limbs.

They swim up to the surface,
Spot targets overhead.
They draw in a few drops,
And shoot 'til they're fed!

The Pistol Shrimp

The ocean is wild!
And in this lawless land,
You might find a small cowboy,
With quite a pistol-like hand.

Just a scurrying shrimp,
He may appear at first.
But not for long once he fires,
His claw with a burst.

He'll sit in his burrow,
As the hours tick past.
But once he sees a small fish,
He'll have to act fast!

He readies his claw,
Brings the hammer far back,
He aims and he fires!
And what a punch it'll pack!

For when his claw snaps,
A tiny bubble blasts out.
The super high pressure,
Stunning all in its route.

It's over in a flash,
And the fish is left still.
So quiet now after,
Such havoc and thrill.

And so crawls the shrimp,
To collect his reward,
For such an excellent shot,
And the bullseye he scored!

Now back to the burrow,
He drags the fish - limp.
In the ocean, a cowboy,
This tiny Pistol Shrimp!

The Tarsier

To survive in the wild,
It helps to have skill.
Flying and swimming,
And sprinting at will.

But often overlooked,
Is a keen sense of sight.
For unlike the others,
It gives an edge at night!

A most impressive example,
Holds tight to a tree,
In the day on his island,
He sleeps away free.

But once comes the darkness,
Once the moon starts to glow,
This creature awakens,
And his true powers show!

Nocturnal in nature,
The Tarsier thrives,
While most others sleep,
He opens his eyes!

And what eyes they are,
As big as can be!
The night's much like day,
When you're able to see!

They do just that,
By being overly-huge,
As they collect what little,
Light can be used.

Not near enough for,
You or me to get by,
But he can hunt through the night,
Thanks to great evolved eyes!

The Mudskipper

Most creatures are content,
With their quite familiar home.
Birds in trees, fish in water,
They rarely choose to roam.

But there will always be the few,
Who will seek out something more,
Who leave the norm and the accepted,
For some strange distant shore.

One such explorer, the Mudskipper,
Is a fish a bit odd and bold,
Refusing life solely in the water,
They truly break the mold!

When they want to feed, escape danger,
Or defend their territory,
They climb up and out, from water to land,
And now they're fish quite free!

They can eat what the other fish can't.
They can move to new tidal pools.
These explorers need only stay wet,
And they're free to break all the rules!

But what keeps them alive,
When they're up on dry land?
And how do they walk,
Without legs, feet, or hands?

Well as long as they're wet,
They can breathe through their skin!
And they move much like us,
But they walk on their fins!

All adventurers need tools to explore,
And the Mudskipper's one to prepare.
From water to land, and back again,
No other fish can compare!

The Pileated Woodpecker

The forest is still,
And the air so quiet.
Then the smack against wood,
And it raises a riot!

A Pileated Woodpecker,
Hammers away!
Holds tight to a tree,
Drills his holes all day!

But all that banging,
Must cause such an ache.
As he chisels the wood,
His head must rattle and shake!

Yet through all the smacks,
This bird's really quite fine,
For he's made his own helmet,
Through great evolution and time.

While he chips on away,
His tongue slips back in his head.
It wraps 'round his own brain,
As a nice cushiony bed!

The soft tongue absorbs,
The powerful hits,
And until he's done pecking,
On his brain it will sit.

This allows him to carve,
A great nest for his brood,
And to hunt for the hidden,
And out of reach food.

Thanks to these helmets,
And the safety they provide,
The Pileated Woodpeckers,
Can peck away and survive!

The Bombardier Beetle

Some bugs may fly,
To escape their doom.
Some bugs may swim,
When predators loom.

Most others may scurry,
At the first dangerous sight,
But some will stand strong,
Who are ready to fight!

The Bombardier Beetle,
Is one such little creature.
When he enters a fight,
He'll use quite a fiery feature!

Deep in his body,
Special substances blend,
Churning and mixing,
Building pressure to send,

Out through the rear,
And toward his attacker,
Acidic and scalding,
It causes disaster!

With a face full of spray,
His attacker will flee.
It'll have learned its harsh lesson.
It'll leave the beetle be.

For the Bombardier Beetle,
Has no need for great jaws.
He'd put to no use,
Any number of claws.

All he needs is his chemistry,
And his chamber inside,
To mix up another batch,
Of his fiery tide!